AF572826

What readers are saying about *Adapt Now:*

"*Adapt Now*'s '77 Rules' should be included as a prerequisite for any leadership development program."

- Mark Hand, Engineering Leader

"Full schedule? No excuses. Set aside time to invest in yourself with *Adapt Now*'s no-nonsense advice."

- Carol Fredrickson, Co-founder of Violence Free and International Speaker

"*Adapt Now* reminded me that inspiration can be contagious when it is introduced correctly."

- Shannon Fleming, Commercial Programs Leader

"To better cope with change in the workplace read *Adapt Now*."

- Melissa Heye, Author and Health Care Leader

"*Adapt Now* is an easy to understand book that is packed full of wisdom. If business leaders would simply read and apply these practical principals they would achieve the great success they desire."

- Joseph Sherren, International Business Strategist and Hall of Fame Speaker

A leadership playbook for growth™

Adapt Now

77 Rules For Rising To The Top Of Any Industry

Kelly Isley

Adapt Now

77 Rules For Rising To
The Top Of Any Industry

kellyisley.the.author@gmail.com
www.AdaptNowBook.com

Published by Tonic Press
Dallas, Texas
www.tonicpress.com

Library of Congress Cataloging-in-Publication Data
Isley, Kelly Adapt Now: 77 Rules for Rising to the Top of Any Industry
ISBN #978-0-9887518-0-4

Book design by Perfect Bound Marketing
Phoenix, Arizona www.PerfectBoundMarketing.com

Part of the Tree Neutral® program, which offsets the number of trees consumed in the production and printing of this book by taking proactive steps, such as planting trees in direct proportion to the number of trees used: www.treeneutral.com

Manufactured in the United States of America
First Edition

To Skip:
My amazing husband who has stolen my heart
and believes in me

To Mitch, Vivian and Natalie:
The young gifted adults that will continue to
make a difference in our world

To my late mother Louise:
An incredible inspiration, teacher, and
political strategist

To my father Arlie and his wife Norma:
The business leader and couple that enjoys life
while giving back

To Bud and Diane:
The power couple who believe in the family

To William Hamm:
My fantastic cousin who told me I could become
an author or anything I wanted to be

Acknowledgements

There are many acknowledgments due when a book represents two decades of experience, effort, and triumph. I would like to begin, however, with special thanks to: Skip Benjes, Mary Ann Zimmerman, Kristin Arnold, Dr. Michael Cofield, Jim Olan Hutcheson, Pamela Jett, Carol Fredrickson, Melissa Lamson, Vivian Benjes, William Hamm, Melissa Brown, Todd Nelson, Vickie Mullins, and Brandi Hollister. Thank you all for helping me bring my ideas alive in the conference room and on the written page.

There are numerous experts who contributed to *Adapt Now* and the research efforts as well. I want to thank them for continuing to add value to the world of business:

- Kathy Dempsey
- Paul Benjes
- Stacy Tetschner
- Shannon Fleming
- Mark Hand
- Pep Katcher
- Saulo Katcher
- Todd Ellinwood
- Paula Mosteller
- David Moniz
- Deborah Gardner
- Meredith Hess
- Elle Hansen
- Chris Rosepapa

Many thanks to all for the unbelievable commitment and tremendous cooperation.

Table of Contents

BUSINESS & ORGANIZATIONS

Introduction

Adapt Now is about uncovering business rules and real world strategies that will clear the path to success for readers in any industry.

My name is Kelly Isley, and I'm leading this exciting adventure along with 15 other sharp business leaders who graciously granted the interviews you will soon be reading.

No matter what brought you here or what you have decided you need to learn from *Adapt Now* – know that you now have *A leadership playbook for growth*™ in hand. A playbook that will help you navigate the ever changing world of business.

Many thanks for joining us.

Aim high,

Kelly

STRATEGY
Future
SUPPORT
Growth

CHAPTER ONE

A Key to Changing the Game

In today's exponential world of business, one week's worth of the Wall Street Journal's contains more content than the average 17th century citizen encounter in a life time. Further, and according to recent analysis of 5 million emails from Baydin, the average email user receives 147 messages per day and deletes 71 (48%) of them. Which means business leaders, their customers, the media, and our nation as a whole, is receiving record amounts of communication on any given day. Communication that could end up buried or lost in translation. So how can leaders be strategic about getting their 'key' communications out today and in the future? Follow along as this leader reveals what your strategic communication plan should include and why it is critical to your growth.

Why

A critical factor that moves an organization from strategy development to implementation is strategic communication. Research tells us that businesses can fail at execution because they neglect the most powerful drivers of effectiveness—decision rights and information flow. Too many businesses and organizations of all sizes, fall into this trap and adopt short term tactics. Tactics that can be fatal.

How To Change The Game

In addition to getting a trusted, unbiased agent to help your company build a strategic communication brief, the following data sets should be constructed by taking these actions:

1. **Recap strategic business goals** – include growth targets, revenue, branding, along with marketing efforts and highlight them. Example: We will expand our product line in the next 12 months by adding 2 new types of running shoes.
2. **Develop 5 key messages** – these are compelling sound bites the business can share both internally & externally with employees, customers, partners, media, and board members.

   Industry examples/key messages

   Annies – Investing in Organic: 123 million pounds of organic ingredients has been purchased by Annie's during fiscal years 2008 – 2012.

   Barnes & Noble – The Barnes & Noble Educator Program is free for K-12 educators. Participants save 20% off list price on all eligible purchases for classroom use, online and in stores.

   Mercedes Benz – As a long-time leader in vehicle safety and innovation, Mercedes-Benz introduces Mercedes-Benz Driving Academy - the first international driving school, with a focus on programs educating teen drivers.

   Target – Since 1946, Target has given 5% of its profit through community grants and programs; today, that giving equals more than $4 million a week.
3. **Identify 5 frequently asked questions** – along with thoughtful, concise answers.
4. **Review relevant media advice and insight** – be prepared for the spotlight by viewing a list of 15 important tips for media interviews in Chapter 3: Lights, Camera, Action!

Leverage

Remember to schedule media training for your leadership team to (closely) follow or run in parallel of your strategic communication planning effort. Studies shows: We retain 10% of what we read. We retain 50% of what we hear and see. We retain 90% of what we do.

OPPORTUNITY

Set up time in the next 3 weeks to get your leadership team together and build or refresh the strategic communication plan.

IMPLEMENT

IMPACT

LEADERSHIP

CHAPTER TWO

Building a Thought Leader

What is the definition of a Thought Leader, their impact on today's world of business, and why will they continue to be important? Let's begin with a simple definition: Thought Leader – a person who is becoming an authority on relevant topics by delivering the answers to the key questions on the minds of their target audience.

Here are five actions today and tomorrow's Thought Leaders will take:

1. Speak at regional and industry conferences in their area of expertise
2. Participate within academic and/or industry research teams and publish results in white paper submissions that support conferences and conventions
3. Expand relationships with the media
4. Submit work and projects to industry competitions
5. Author textbooks and/or study guides for university-level audiences

How can you get started?

Look ahead 2–12 months and fulfill white paper opportunities or contribute details supporting a "call for speakers" request to key regional or industry conferences. Continue building or adding to media relationships by commenting on op-editorials or popular blogs that journalists in your industry monitor. Follow that by identifying, assembling, and sending in your work for noteworthy awards that can capture significant visibility. Feeling ambitious and enjoy writing? Look for a university professor who is interested in co-authoring a study or book in your areas of expertise. If you want to get started right away: set up a blog showcasing your great content or submit an article to a local media group for evaluation and make the commitment to publish twice a month.

OPPORTUNITY

Which of the five actions above can you tackle in the next 14 days? Identify one in the next seven days and monitor how it positively impacts your relationship and credibility with business colleagues along with other members of your leadership team.

IMPLEMENT

____

____

____

____

____

____

____

____

IMPACT

CHAPTER THREE

Lights, Camera, Action!

Let's set the scene: you have recently completed media training, your public relations manager has captured an opportunity for you to appear on television later this week, and you have been given advance questions. So, what do you do now?

Prepare

How can you get started? Begin with reviewing a proven check list that this leader has used to prepare several executives for their moments in the television spot light and for my own interviews:

1. Keep in mind that if you are anywhere near a camera, it is a good assumption that it is on and recording every word and action.
2. Always ask the reporter what the topic is for the story in advance. Find out if it is impromptu (and, if possible)—before the cameras start rolling.
3. Remember that you must convert your message points into sound bites.*
4. Do not wear stripes; they dance around on the screen and are distracting. Solid bright colors look best: reds, bright blues, and shades of green.
5. Keep in mind that people shouldn't judge you by your appearance, but they will, and having a neat, professional suit/uniform/dress is important.

6. Avoid doing, or wearing, anything distracting on TV—people will remember that and nothing you say.
7. As a reminder, every TV anchorman, soap opera actor, sitcom star, and talk show host on TV is made up and groomed for TV. Unfortunately, this is the TV audience's standard of comparison when they are watching you.
8. Do not look at the camera unless there is no reporter or host around to speak to.
9. Avoid leaning back in your chair; (if seated) you will appear short and heavy.
10. Resist sitting up perfectly straight; you'll look stiff and nervous.
11. Do lean forward 15 degrees into the camera; you'll look taller, leaner, and more confident.
12. By leaning forward, you gain another advantage—any hint of a double chin will disappear and you will appear to have a stronger jaw line.
13. Moving your body (slightly) is positive.
14. Do move your hands—whoever told speakers not to use their hands was not given accurate information.
15. Do not move your hands above your face, below your chest, or wider than your shoulder.

* *Your key messages will remain relevant when they are reviewed every 3–6 months.*

OPPORTUNITY

What steps will you take to prepare for your moment in the television spotlight? Remember to set aside time to role-play any advanced questions and review your top five key messages prior to a media interview.

IMPLEMENT

IMPACT

CHAPTER FOUR

Resiliency: A Leader's Secret Weapon

Resilient leaders leave their mark on the future, just as they shape history. Despite changing economies they bounce back and manage to stay focused while moving their businesses forward. How can we learn from their successes? To find the answers, I sat down with Mary Ann Zimmerman, author, LPC, LISAC, and accomplished business leader to address these questions:

Q · What is your definition of a resilient leader?

Ms. Zimmerman · *Resilience is often described as a learnable mindset that predisposes us to "bounce back" in the face of loss or adversity. Resilient leaders, however, do more than bounce back—they bounce, and in certain cases, leap forward. They respond to new challenges, even as they maintain the routine operations of the organizations they lead. In addition, resilient leaders quickly get a second wind, and when they see that the status quo is not optimal, they use it to move mountains and build remarkable organizations.*

Q · Is resiliency a critical trait for leaders of today and tomorrow?

Ms. Zimmerman · *Resiliency has been a critical trait for leaders throughout history. In fact, if you look at leaders in any field of endeavor, whether business or political, we find that many have experienced tremendous setbacks, suffered great adversity, and yet never succumbed for long. Eventually,* *they overcame their challenges, and went on to great achievements. Examples include Abraham Lincoln who battled severe clinical depression, Martin Luther King who overcame tremendous obstacles to lead the country in a better direction, or Steve Jobs who coped with cancer as he created one of the greatest companies in the world.*

Q · What advantages do resilient leaders deliver to their businesses and organizations?

Ms. Zimmerman · *Though there are many advantages, two in particular come to mind, and involve recognized leaders whose companies touch our daily lives.*

First, ***resilient leaders model resilient behavior to other employees.*** *In essence, they serve as an inspiration as others see how resilient leaders deal with adversity, overcome challenges, and move forward in spite of these instances. One such leader is Howard Schultz who regained his position as Starbucks CEO in 2008.*

In the darkest days of the recession, many analysts and media outlets had written Starbucks off. However, armed with a positive mind-set and a business mantra which always challenge the old ways, Mr. Schultz returned financial discipline, bottom-line efficiency, and a back-to-basics focus to the company.

For example, the company had been losing tens of millions of dollars a year by pouring excess steamed milk down the drain. By simply putting a serrated internal ring inside a pitcher to guide how much milk a barista can use for a latte, Starbucks saved millions. As with Steve Jobs at Apple, Starbuck's second act, led by Howard Schultz, turned the company's iconic brand around.

And second, ***resilient leaders tend to be more optimistic and purposeful.*** *This can lead to a positive emotional "contagion" effect on a work team, and cause other team members to get "caught up" in the energy that results.*

One leading practitioner of empowerment management, John Mackey, the co-CEO of Whole Foods Market, Inc. believes that purpose inspires people. This has been his belief since opening his first food store in 1978, and has helped build his business into a $10 billion Fortune 500 company that is now one of the top supermarket firms in America.

Q • What are three good tips you can share and that leaders can use immediately to boost their resiliency?

Ms. Zimmerman • *Initially, leaders need to familiarize themselves with the benefits of resilience learning, and do a careful self-analysis to gain some perspective. The formula is:*

> **Resilient Strength = Understanding Your Strengths + Understanding Your Weaknesses**

Next, leaders need to immerse themselves in the subject of learned optimism. The research shows that rational, learned optimism, like any other attribute and skill, can be cultivated.

Optimism is one of the single greatest predictors of resilience, and is correlated highly with positive outcomes in virtually every field of human endeavor. Consider the following quote from Dean Becker, the President and CEO of Adaptiv Learning Systems in Harvard Business Review: "More than education, more than experience, more than training, a person's level of resilience will determine who succeeds and who fails. That's true in the cancer ward, it's true in the Olympics, and it's true in the boardroom."

Finally, leaders need to learn some concrete tools, and then take action. Understanding resiliency abstractly is a necessary but insufficient condition for success. Many of the resiliency building tools available to individuals and companies are simple to implement, but must be practiced on a regular basis in order to take effect.

OPPORTUNITY

Who will you inspire with your optimistic outlook today? Identify one person inside your business or organization that has inspired you or others, and thank them for it.

IMPLEMENT

IMPACT

Ideas

CHAPTER FIVE

Doctor's Orders

Before traveling, consider scanning your documents (e.g., passports, traveler's identity, allergies, vaccination records, plus other important information) and sending them to your primary email address. If you run into a problem, you can have them printed out at a local internet café or hotel business center or they can be viewed on a smart phone.

If the forecast calls for a full travel schedule, remember to download the email/information into your smart phone as an attachment, so it will be available to you even if network coverage is not.

Two additional resources plus one clever app worth reviewing include: 1) the Smart Traveler app by the U.S. State Department, which can be downloaded for free on iTunes. This iPhone app invites you to see the world with easy access to frequently updated official country information, travel alerts, travel warnings, maps, U.S. embassy locations, and much more; 2) enroll in the Smart Traveler Enrollment Program (STEP) on the U.S. Department of State website, which will help in case of an emergency or if challenges are encountered; 3) bookmark and become familiar with the important sections on the international travel portion of the U.S. Department of State website, which has outlined tips for traveling abroad and current travel warnings, together with travel alerts.

OPPORTUNITY

Scan your important travel documents, email them to yourself, and download them on your smart phone.

IMPLEMENT

IMPACT

Ideas

CHAPTER SIX

Seven Smart Moves To Make Before Attending A Conference

For every leader who has a full schedule and must attend important conferences, my seven recommendations for maximizing your time follow:

1. **Identify two key people you want to meet during the conference and do it.** This may include: potential clients, candidates for strategic partnership, new members, the keynote speaker, possible mentors, or a host of others who you can connect with and that may help move you closer to your goals.

2. **Build an elevator speech or update your current one.** Sharpen your 20 – 30 second speech that explains your role and expertise.

3. **Contact those covering the press for the conference in advance and please coordinate your efforts with any PR representatives that you or your company may work with.** When you get your conference agenda, review it and identify the main sponsor that will cover and issue press during the conference.

4. **Stay at the host hotel if possible and stay during the key days.** Even though this is not school and you can easily arrive late and leave early, you never know what you might be missing by doing this.

5. **Give and *get* business cards.** Make sure you take plenty of your business cards. Also when you receive business cards, write short descriptions on the back when you get a break and

follow up as appropriate. It may also be wise to bring key sales material printed or (eco- friendly) via thumb drives.

6. **Be an active participant, not a passive observer.** You may not be a formal presenter, but that doesn't mean you don't have something to contribute. Make sure you ask intelligent/relevant questions and make comments when the format allows it.
7. **When entering a large conference stay near the back until you identify your key people to contact and position yourself accordingly.** This is what you will see the 'connectors' doing and most often key leadership will stay near the back of a conference if they are not speaking and for exiting purposes.

OPPORTUNITY

Identify a keynote speaker or significant contributor and secure a time to meet them for coffee, before the next conference gets underway.

IMPLEMENT

IMPACT

CHAPTER SEVEN

Bottom line: The Cost of an Unhappy Work Force and How to Fix It

Today we see alarming reports that lost productivity, from actively disengaged employees, is costing the U.S. economy $370 billion annually. If you are a leader wondering how widespread this "disengaging" crisis is and what steps you can take to win this battle in your own company, follow along as I interview Pamela Jett, MS, CSP, global business communications expert, and author of an important new book on the subject.

Q · The new book, "Communicate to Keep 'Em", seems to have struck a good balance of business acumen, storytelling, and science. How did the book develop and why did you release it this fall?

Ms. Jett · *The book was written because we have entered a worldwide disengagement crisis. How big is the challenge we are facing? Research tells us that barely one in five employees in the U.S. are engaged on the job and the rest fall into some category of disengagement. Looking through a global lens, unsettling estimates indicate that only 11% of employees are actively engaged in their jobs today. Case in point, during recent business meetings in Asia, I met leaders who expressed concerns regarding their countries' disengaged workforces along with how the trend has impacted business growth.*

Next, and based on the large economic impact, it is a relevant book for companies that want to move their work force from "disengaged" to "engaged"—the engaged and productive employees who can spur business growth.

Q • You mentioned previewing the new book in Asia; was it well received?

Ms. Jett • *Absolutely. In Singapore, the Human Resources professionals appreciated the focus on practical application, language patterns (that can help bilingual employees), and specific "words to choose" and "words to lose," which has helped them discover communication tools that they have put to work immediately.*

Q • Can you share three tips that readers can use right away?

Ms. Jett • *Of course. Here is* ***Tip No. 1: Eliminate the word "should."*** *Why? If you stop "should-ing" on people (e.g., "you should do this . . ." or "you shouldn't do it that way; you should do it like this . . ."), you will stop using a disengaging form of communication. First and foremost, professionals do not appreciate it when others try to "tell them what to do" and deny them their freedom to choose.*

So, instead of using "you should," consider the power of replacing it with one of these options:

- *It would be better if you did it this way . . .*
- *The _______ (project, employee handbook, contract) requires you to do it this way . . .*
- *Our _______ (customer, bottom line) benefits when you do it this way . . .*

Next, ***Tip No. 2: Ditch the word "Don't" and focus on what you would like them to do instead.*** *Here are two classic examples—replace "Don't be late" with "Please be on time" or replace "Don't forget . . ." with "Please remember . . ." These are both good examples of sharing what the desired behavior is as opposed to the undesired behavior.*

Lastly, I want to share one of my favorites in **Tip No. 3: Ask open-ended questions.** *Why is this important? Because using open-ended questions is one of the easiest tools anyone at any level of the organization can use, and they are also one of the most effective forms of engaging communication. Here are a few of my top open-ended questions:*

- *What are your thoughts on this?*
- *How do you think this will benefit _______ (the team, our customer, the bottom line)?*
- *How can this be done _______ (better, smarter, faster, more efficiently)?*

I have found that by integrating these and other open-ended questions into my global clients' regular communication, they are viewed as more open, approachable, and respectful individuals.

Q ▪ Excellent tips. Now, from your perspective, who can benefit from this new book?

Ms. Jett ▪ *Job titles and positions aside, every one of us can benefit from the new book. Why? Because each of us can make a positive impact on employee engagement using the most important skill set we have—our communication skills. We can each choose to make changes that positively affect ourselves, those we lead, and our peers—changes that can result in happier, more productive companies.*

OPPORTUNITY

What open-ended question will you ask today? Identify a set of five open-ended questions to ask this week and evaluate the responses to see how they have positively impacted your engagement with team members and business colleagues.

IMPLEMENT

IMPACT

Ideas

CHAPTER EIGHT

Calm, Cool and Collected

Could a negative email or damaging blog post cost you or your company more than wasted time and emotion? Absolutely. To avoid this situation and before you hit "send" or "post," please ask yourself one question: "Would I want to see this published in the newspaper, company newsletter, or on the 'Huffington Post'?" If the answer is "no," hit the delete key and save your time for productive tasks that will improve your bottom line—instead of adding risk to it.

Another approach to handling surprise criticism follows. Whether it is a critic received directly or indirectly, Peter Bregman's experience and his popular column for Harvard Business Review suggest four steps:

1. Look beyond your feelings.
2. Look beyond their delivery.
3. Don't agree or disagree. Just collect the data.
4. Later, with some distance, decide what you want to do.

In Mr. Bregman's words, "Criticism can be an incredible gift, a field guide for acting with impact in the world. All we need is enough patience and presence to read it."

OPPORTUNITY

Identify the easiest way for you to handle surprise criticism in the future.

IMPLEMENT

IMPACT

Ideas

CHAPTER NINE

When Capital Is King

Having a solid understanding of the capital budgeting process is critical from an intellectual standpoint. It is also vital for leaders to grasp how a business can and will create future value by leveraging capital investments. The world's greatest executives – Warren Buffett at Berkshire Hathaway, Herb Kelleher of Southwest Airlines, Jack Welch at General Electric, and Richard Branson of the Virgin Group – have a long history of making value-creating decisions. These leaders have a thorough understanding of the capital budgeting process.

Benefits

Capital budgeting creates a structured step-by-step process that enables a company to:

1. Formulate and develop long-term strategic goals – the ability to set long-term goals is essential to the growth and prosperity of any business. The ability to appraise/value investment projects via capital budgeting creates a framework for businesses to plan out future long-term direction.
2. Identify and evaluate new investment projects – knowing how to evaluate investment projects gives a business the model to seek, prioritize, and assess new projects, an important function for all businesses as they seek to compete and profit in their industry.
3. Forecast and estimate future cash flows – future cash flows are what create value for businesses over time. Capital budgeting

enables leaders to take a potential project and estimate its future cash flows, which then helps determine if such a project should be accepted.

4. Transfer of information – from the time that a project starts off as an idea, until the time it is accepted or rejected, numerous decisions have to be made at various levels of authority. The capital budgeting process facilitates the transfer of information to the appropriate decision makers within a company.
5. Control of Expenditures – by definition a budget carefully identifies the necessary expenditures along with research and development (R&D) required for an investment project. Since a good project can turn bad if expenditures are not carefully controlled or monitored, this step is a crucial benefit of the capital budgeting process.
6. Creation of Decision – when a capital budgeting process is in place, a company is then able to create a set of decision rules that can categorize which projects are acceptable and which projects are unacceptable. The result is a more efficiently run business that is better equipped to quickly adapt to the dynamic world of business.

In addition to a financial decision, a company is also making an investment in its future direction and growth that will likely have an influence on future projects that the company considers and evaluates. So to make a capital investment decision only from the perspective of either a financial or investment decisions can pose serious limitations on the success of the project.

Industry Case Study

In December 2009 ExxonMobil, the world's largest oil company, announced that it was acquiring XTO Resources, one of the largest natural gas companies in the U.S. for $41 billion. That acquisition was a capital budgeting decision, one in which ExxonMobil made a huge financial commitment. Additionally, ExxonMobil was making a significant investment decision in natural gas and essentially positioning the company to also focus on growth opportunities in the natural gas arena. That acquisition alone will have a profound effect on future projects that ExxonMobil considers and evaluates for many years to come.

The significance of these dual decisions is profound for companies. Leaders have been known to lose jobs over poor investment decisions. One can say that running a business is nothing more than a constant exercise in capital budgeting decisions. Understanding that both a financial and investment decision is being made is the key to making successful capital investment decisions in any business environment.

Capital Budgeting Decision Tools

Once projects have been identified, management then begins the financial process of determining whether or not the project should be pursued. The three common capital budgeting decision tools are the payback period, net present value (NPV) method and the internal rate of return (IRR) method.

Payback Period

The payback period is the most basic and simple decision tool. With this method, you are determining how long it will take to pay back the initial investment that is required to undergo a project. In order to calculate this, you would take the total cost of the project and divide it by how much cash inflow you expect to receive each year; this will give you the total number of years or the payback period. For example, if you are considering buying a coffee shop that is selling for $100,000 and that coffee shop produces cash flows of $20,000 a year, the payback period is five years.

Net Present Value (NPV)

The net present value decision tool is a more common and more effective process of evaluating a project. Perform a net present value calculation essentially requires calculating the difference between the project cost (cash outflows) and cash flows generated by that project (cash inflows). The NPV tool is effective since it uses discounted cash flow analysis, where future cash flows are discounted at a discount rate to compensate for the uncertainty of those future cash flows. The term "present value" in NPV refers to the fact that cash flows earned in the future are not worth as much as cash flows today. Discounting those future cash flows back to the present creates an apples-to-apples comparison between the cash flows. The difference provides you with the net present value.

Internal Rate of Return (IRR)

The internal rate of return is a discount rate that is commonly used to determine how much of a return an investor can expect to realize from a particular project. Strictly defined, the internal rate of return is the discount rate that occurs when a project is break even, or when the NPV equals 0. Here, the decision rule is simple: choose the project where the IRR is higher than the cost of financing. In other words, if your cost of capital is 5%, you do not accept projects unless the IRR is greater than 5%. The greater the difference between the financing cost and the IRR, the more attractive the project becomes.

Capital budgeting decision tools, like any other business formula, are certainly not perfect barometers, but IRR is a highly-effective concept that serves its purpose in the investment decision making process.

OPPORTUNITY

Set up time in the next 21 days to get your leadership team together and build or refresh the businesses capital plan.

IMPLEMENT

____

____

____

IMPACT

CHAPTER TEN

Succession Planning: Who Will Be Next?

Leadership departures stole headlines and became a recurring theme with the S&P 500 CEO's in 2012. Was the damage worse than we thought? According to a Harvard Law study: CEO Succession Practices (2013 Edition); 31.4% of all successions were non-voluntary departures in 2012, the highest rate recorded since 2003. Is this a sign that corporate boards must be more proactive about (and simply better at handling) leadership succession? Could the lack of planning be impacting businesses of all sizes? To get the answers, I sat down with James Olan Hutcheson, founder of ReGENERATION Partners, award-winning author, contributing editor, and influential keynote speaker. Interview highlights that include Mr. Hutcheson's sound advice follow.

Q · How much of the leadership team should be considered in succession planning? Is it important to plan beyond the CEO position?

Mr. Hutcheson · *Successful businesses evaluate the skills and attitudes of everyone inside and outside the organization who is a candidate for a leadership position. Everyone? Yes, because the CEO isn't the only position that requires succession planning. As an example, if a company suddenly loses its chief technology officer, chief financial officer, or another key player - that departure can potentially carry the impact of an unexpected vacancy in the president's office.*

Q • This is good advice regarding an evaluation of both inside and outside candidates. In your experience who is the better leadership candidate?

Mr. Hutcheson • *Based on two decades of experience, our firm has learned there is no single, right way to install an inside or outside heir as the leader of a business, any more than there is a single wrong approach. Research confirms this along with our first-hand knowledge supporting the fact that: current board members can be very successful CEO candidates.*

Building on evidence based research - Spencer Stuart, a global executive search firm, conducted an 18-month study of the 300 CEO transitions at S&P 500 companies that took place from 2004 to 2008, delivering results that contained several surprises. Contrary to conventional wisdom, their analysis showed that insiders and outsiders have performed about the same—plenty of each fell into the highest and lowest performance categories. Whether a company chose a CEO from inside or outside did matter—but whether the choice turned out to be wise depended mostly on the health and competitive position of the company at the time of succession.

Q • Very Interesting. What else?

Mr. Hutcheson • *Well, another surprising finding in their study is that: Board members who stepped in as CEO's outperformed all other types of candidates. In many cases, a board member is a last resort, someone who is turned to in desperation when a company can't find other suitable candidates. In reality, directors-turned-CEOs represent a strong blend of insider and outsider. They have more company knowledge than a pure outsider, while they don't have the constraints of a pure insider when it comes to making unpopular decisions or leading painful changes. Having been on the board, they have deep knowledge of a company's strategy, finances, and organization, and just as important, they understand the* *dynamics and the expectations of the board. And of course, some have already been CEOs of other companies, which has a distinct advantage.*

Conversely, the studies worst performing CEOs turned out to be a group we call insider-outsiders: outsiders who are hired into a company as president or chief operating officer and promoted to CEO within 18 months. HR directors have favored this approach, and in theory it makes great sense. The candidate has a chance to get acclimated to the culture, learn the company, and settle in before ascending to the top job. But the approach often sets the new leader up for failure.

Q • Why so?

Mr. Hutcheson • *The two-step succession process requires the candidate to "audition" for the top position while serving under the incumbent CEO, and that tends to makes him or her beholden to the current chief executive. What's more, the sitting CEO remains the primary conduit to the board—making it more likely that the outside hire will play things safe and be deferential to the status quo. Ten insider-outsider CEOs were appointed between 2004 and 2008, and our analysis found that none of them achieved top-quartile performance.*

Further, the research also found that many of the criteria boards use to evaluate CEO candidates turn out to be unimportant in predicting performance. These include candidates' ages, where they went to college or grad school, what degrees they earned, whether they needed to relocate or commute to take the job, or whether they began their career at a blue-chip company. Boards should ignore those variables; they simply don't correlate with performance.

Based on our experience at ReGENERATION Partners and the study, the most important factor in determining which type of CEO candidate to select is the health of the company.

Insiders are best when the company is performing well; outsiders tend to do better when the company is in crisis. Although this may be intuitive, when this data has been shown to board members, they're surprised by how compelling the numbers are.

Q • How can the decision makers capture reliable information about the abilities and competencies of each successor candidate?

Mr. Hutcheson • *Here are three successful strategies that we use at our firm:*

1. *Assign a trusted member of the leadership team to mentor the top candidates and bring in a respected outside expert to give a realistic assessment of his/her performance potential.*
2. *Place final candidates in charge of a short-term (3 – 6 months) "special project" for which you*

want to see measurable results.

3. *Transition top candidates to a position with clearly defined performance goals for which s/he would be accountable within 9 months.*

OPPORTUNITY

Does your company have a succession planning process in place that could be refreshed? Is the company looking at leadership changes or promotions within the next 18 months? If the answer is yes to either of these scenarios, identify three business strategies for improvement and implement them within the next 30 days.

IMPLEMENT

IMPACT

CHAPTER ELEVEN

Unproductive Meetings: How to Avoid the Great White Collar Crime

When Industry Week called meetings "the Great White Collar Crime," estimating they waste $37 billion a year, it captured the spotlight and studies kicked off to see what was behind the damage in North America. Research conducted by the Annenberg School of Communications at UCLA and the University of Minnesota's Training & Development Research Center showed executives on average spend 40–50% of their working hours in meetings. Further, the studies point out that as much as 50% of meeting time is unproductive and that up to 25% is spent discussing irrelevant issues. Worse, results indicated 9 out of 10 people daydream in meetings. If you are looking for a solution to this business challenge, join my interview with Kristin Arnold, an award-winning business author and industry leader to watch. We gain insight from her credentials spanning 20 years that include: founder and president of The Extraordinary Team & QPC Inc., past president of the U.S. National Speakers Association as well as one of the leading high stakes meeting facilitators for global clients.

Q · Ms. Arnold, is it true that unproductive meetings can negatively impact the bottom line of businesses today?

Ms. Arnold · *Yes, indeed. Other research, including a teamwork study from the University of Arizona, indicates there are more than 11 million formal meetings per day in the United States—adding up to three billion meetings per year. Managers spend about 20% of their time in formal meetings of 5 people or more and a meeting between several* *managers or executives may cost upwards of $1000 per hour in salary costs alone. As a point of reference, a single Fortune 50 company estimates losses in excess of $75 million per year due to poor meetings.*

Based on these findings, it is clear that team meetings deserve attention and have room for improvement in many of today's businesses.

Q • If you were working with a team that needs to get back on the productive meeting track quickly, what advice would you give them?

Ms. Arnold • *Here are six actions that team leaders can take that will help them regain productivity right away:*

1. ***Check your alignment** – Make sure every attendee knows the overall goal (rarely is a meeting not connected to a larger objective), meeting purpose, the deliverable, and specific measurable targets in advance.*
2. ***Ask yourself, "Do I really have to do this?"** – Is the targeted outcome something that can be accomplished during a quick face-to-face exchange or a series of phone calls?*
3. ***Leverage technology** – Fully utilize today's technology that can streamline everything from scheduling and recording to information sharing without leaving your desktop. Examples inside of Microsoft Office include: Lync and Outlook, along with SharePoint. Outside solutions for engagement can be covered by Skype, Doodle, and Google Docs.*
4. ***Share the agenda** – Oddly, independent studies indicate that up to 60% of meetings do not have prepared agendas. Embrace this simple step and make your agenda as specific as possible. Alternatively, if the meeting starts out without an agenda, be bold and create one at the beginning of the meeting. Use this simple formula: List*

the topics/name, ask how long/who will lead, does the team have enough time? If no—assign A-B-C priorities, and start with the "A's."

5. **Wear one hat at a time** – *Remember that in team management three prevalent scenarios include: hierarchical; team based; and self-directed models. Your role changes as a leader, facilitator, and team member. Stay focused on your role and lead based on which model is assigned to the project at hand. This avoids confusion along with duplicated effort as the team moves forward.*
6. **Create and track action items** – *Before wrapping up, make sure action items are summarized, and that roles along with due dates are assigned to each participant. If a follow-on meeting is critical, schedule it before the group breaks up also. Working with a large team? Consider a revolving action item list (RAIL) that is typically built in Excel with these headings: action, owner, description, priority, open date, and finish date.*

OPPORTUNITY

Which meeting are you leading this week that can be more productive? Identify three of the actions above and implement them within the next seven days.

IMPLEMENT

____

____

____

____

IMPACT

Ideas

CHAPTER TWELVE

It Is Business - Not Personal

Successful team members know that personalizing things that are not personal and holding grudges is a waste of time and energy. Although having a caring persona is an advantage for today's team members and leaders in many business situations, those same savvy men and women know that in business, there is actually less personal conflict than people imagine. So the next time an isolated comment or missed connection enters the picture—consider giving that person the benefit of the doubt and move forward.

Two other advantages team members will gain by viewing the conflict as professional versus personal: 1) avoid accidently overreacting and imagining a personal component that did not exist and 2) positively dilute any personal conflict that may have existed.

In the end, avoiding a personal war and refusing to let someone drag you or your team into one, is the best way to stay on the high road—the same high road that leads to the fast track.

OPPORTUNITY

What grudge can you or your team eliminate today? Identify 2 per team member, spend 10 minutes (or less) writing down the history, dedicate another 5 minutes on how you can give that person the benefit of the doubt or forgive them, and make the decision to move forward without the weight of that grudge on your shoulders.

IMPLEMENT

IMPACT

Ideas

TEAM MEETING
Meeting called by:
Facilitator:
Timekeeper:

CHAPTER THIRTEEN

Producing Results in Every Economy

Proven approach: Meeting attendees should include a cross section of the team with the most senior member as the facilitator. At a minimum, have leaders from customer service or customer programs, finance, and operations ready to deliver concise updates that tie to the annual business goals.

Adapting for today's workforce could dictate that members attend virtually (e.g., web conferencing, video conference, via speaker phone, et al.). Reminder: designate a scribe to capture decisions and actions. If administrative assistance is at a premium, consider rotating this role. And to keep momentum moving forward, make sure that the meeting notes are distributed within 24 hours.

Next, gain priority on schedules by making this a meeting that team members look forward to attending by "breaking news." A good newsworthy practice: introduce important internal news or a relevant industry sound bite (from the headlines) at the beginning of the meeting and move quickly around the room or through the agenda.

OPPORTUNITY

Schedule a reoccurring, mandatory team meeting within the next 10 days that includes a good cross section of the organization. Do you already hold a weekly meeting? Look for ways to optimize the format and content by tapping into your team for suggestions.

IMPLEMENT

IMPACT

Ideas

CHAPTER FOURTEEN

The Losada Ratio: Predicting Success

It is true that productive teams can turn companies around. But how do you build or reshape a team to be successful? To discover how, I secured a rare interview with the knowledgeable Dr. Michael Cofield, Diplomate in Clinical Health Psychology with the American Board of Professional Psychology. Highlights that introduce the Losada Ratio and related, successful strategies follow:

Q · What is the "Losada Line" and how can it be a strategic tool for work teams?

Dr. Cofield · *The Losada Ratio was developed by a well-known organizational psychologist, Dr. Marcial Losada. He studied over fifty companies, utilizing verbatim transcripts of strategic planning meetings. He discovered that the most successful companies have a predictable three to one ratio of positive to negative interactions between team members. That is, for every critical interaction, there needs to be at least three positive ones in order to offset the negativity. Companies that fell below 3:1 P/N (positive/negative ratio) were shown to function much more poorly in terms of productivity and profit. Thus, increasing a company's P/N can yield huge benefits.*

Q · What types of advantages can work teams that fall within the optimum zone deliver to their business and organizations?

Dr. Cofield • Well, one example is a mining company that Losada's group worked with and reported on. The company was losing a significant degree of productivity and profit every month. However, once some relatively simple "P/N" strategies were implemented amongst the managers, they saw a 40% increase in productivity at the end of the year. The company's CEO wrote an extremely grateful letter praising the organizational intervention efforts and giving them great credit for essentially turning the company's productivity around.

Q • What are one or two good strategies work teams can use immediately to get closer to the optimum ratio, and will stand the test of time?

Dr. Cofield • *One technique that has been utilized is the implementation of an "E-ppreciation" strategy. Each team member is asked to write a very brief message of appreciation to a different team member on a daily basis, or at least three times per week.*

Secondly, a very effective communication strategy known as "DPR" or Dynamic Positive Responding, teaches team members and supervisors how to "celebrate" good news, rather than focusing exclusively on negative input.

Q • What is a good resource that work teams can use to monitor when they want to gain a deeper understanding of this area or monitor what is on the horizon?

Dr. Cofield • *One excellent website is "AuthenticHappiness.com". It contains a variety of self-assessment tools free of charge. They measure such success-related workplace attributes as personal optimism and "grit" or the tendency to "stick to it" on the job, regardless of the challenges.*

OPPORTUNITY

Do you have a team that can benefit from one of these techniques? If so, have the team report progress, within the first two months of their effort to keep the momentum going.

IMPLEMENT

IMPACT

CHAPTER FIFTEEN

What Can We Learn from a Lizard?

When *Fortune Magazine* found that workplace learning was a common thread in the "100 Best Companies to Work For," leaders took notice. Building on that news (and turbulent economy) this leader started the search for change management learning opportunities that were unique, yet proven. Imagine my surprise when a highly recommended program included a subject matter expert named: Lenny T. Lizard. Yes, a lizard! Intrigued, I contacted Lenny's business partner, Kathy Dempsey, President of Keep Shedding! Inc., to learn more. As it turned out, Ms. Dempsey, an award winning author, keynote speaker and recognized "change expert", has worked with several Fortune 500 companies. Her goal: to implement programs that ignite change in leaders. Follow along in our interview that covers lessons you will enjoy.

Q · **What is the philosophy of shedding? Why is this important and how did Lenny become your business partner?**

Ms. Dempsey · *Good questions and let's start with Lenny. As background, Lenny was the result of a life-changing conversation with a colleague about his pet lizard that died because it didn't shed his skin. Two transformational things happened that day: first he gave me a benchmark for my personal growth path so I had a metaphor "shed or you're dead" featuring Lenny who has been a great listener, business partner, and vehicle for helping people. Second, it* *is remarkable how much lizards can teach us about growth and change. One key lesson from tomorrow's business professionals and organizations is that if they don't shed they can become unhealthy and die.*

Q • Fantastic introduction. Can you tell us- what is the biggest barrier to shedding in today's world of business?

Ms. Dempsey • *Overcoming fear is the biggest barrier to shedding. Studies teach us that a staggering 95% of people say that fear is the number one thing that holds them back at work and in life.*

A few years ago I had the privilege of speaking for the Disney Corporation in Orlando. After experiencing an incredible backstage tour I was surprised to discover that Walt Disney was afraid of mice.

So what did he do to face his fear? He embraced that fear and transformed it into his biggest professional success. Walt Disney chose to make his fear less scary. He added big ears, a fun playful face and named his fear: Mickey.

***The key lesson:** when you resist facing your fear there is usually a price to pay - not only to you but also to others.*

Just think for a moment, if Walt Disney had never faced his fear - there would be no Disney World. Can you imagine the millions of people being robbed of their happy childhood memories and family vacations?

Q • Fascinating. Can you share a few more lessons that can help leaders in their quest to conquer change management?

Ms. Dempsey • *Definitely. Here are three lessons.*

1. ***Heighten your awareness.***
   It is the key to any behavioral change. A good example of this would be learning to manage your energy, not your time. Your energy is critical for sustaining success.

2. ***Take a recharge break every 90 minutes.***
   Research shows that in workplaces where regular breaks are encouraged, productivity increases and rates of sickness decrease.

3. ***Focus your energy on things you can control or influence.***
   Why? Ask yourself - where do most of us waste our energy? On things we have no control over. A good reminder: make a conscious effort not to let control issues rob you of your precious time and energy. Instead, strive to focus only on the things that you have control over today.

OPPORTUNITY

Which fear can you embrace in the next 10 days? Keep in mind that the cure for fear is – action. How can you take a page from Walt Disney's life and make that fear your friend?

IMPLEMENT

IMPACT

Ideas

CHAPTER SIXTEEN

Time Is More Than Money

Make sure your company's name is heard this year by issuing strategic news releases, through the marketing/PR team, that arrive at the right time and tie to current events, holidays, or important milestones. As your team plans releases for the year ahead, strongly consider the timing. If the press or news release is strategic versus urgent, avoid the time around the open and close of the stock market. Public companies tend to issue releases at both the market's open and close, resulting in a tidal wave of announcements that can overshadow your news.

Additionally, there are four windows throughout the year when public companies report earnings, and reporters, especially business reporters, tend to focus on earnings ahead of all other events. These quarterly periods are:

- January 15 through February 15
- April 15 through May 15
- July 15 through August 15
- October 15 through November 15

OPPORTUNITY

Arrange for your marketing and/or PR team to take note and multiply the value of every news release scheduled in your next two months.

Track progress, and report visibility statistics, et al., on the releases each quarter to senior leadership.

IMPLEMENT

IMPACT

Ideas

5
55
50
45
40
35
60
10
50
20
40
30

CHAPTER SEVENTEEN

The Business of Competition

How will tomorrow's leaders win the battle against their competition? Can the battles be won if businesses continue the focus on customers? Will the business world still favor speed in the future? For answers to these questions, I sat down with Deborah Gardner, award-winning athlete, recognized author, and competitive performance expert to learn more. Our interview highlights follow.

Q · Will customer focus be enough to keep the competition at bay for tomorrow's business leaders?

Ms. Gardner · *Customer focus is the place to start. According to a study by The Wharton School, stakes are high as reducing customer attrition by 5 to 10% can increase annual profits as much as 75%. The take away: invest in your customer programs and service groups. They can be the first face or voice your customers reach and the reason your customers stay.*

Q · How can tomorrow's leaders identify trends that will change the game early, so you can quickly build on their momentum?

Ms. Gardner · *Great question, here are four tactics that are working well and can stand the test of time:*

1. ***Expand your services*** *– this will make it harder for customers to move and counter any balance of power opportunities your team may encounter.*

2. ***Leverage technology*** – *the business world will continue to reward speed and abundance. Tap into the latest technology that can speed up your entry to market. A good example from manufacturing is the 3-D printing capability which is revolutionizing one of the nation's oldest industries.*

3. ***Raise the price of admission*** – *keep new competing businesses out of your targeted area by investing in research and development or other areas that directly add value to your offerings while leveling the playing field.*

4. ***Increase potential supplier base*** – *move away from customization towards standardization when possible. This can open the door across several vendors/suppliers versus a select few.*

OPPORTUNITY

Which tactic or strategy can you embrace in the next 21 days that will slow the competitions progress?

IMPLEMENT

____

____

____

____

____

____

IMPACT

6
7
8
9
9
8
7
6
5

CHAPTER EIGHTEEN

How to Price Goods and Services So Clients Will Buy Them

For many businesses, one of the most difficult questions to answer is: "How do we price our products and services? So how do company leaders answer this question? Many of them start by looking at the competition to see who has been successful and at what price. This approach is certainly a good place to begin. But what else can companies do to make sure they price their products good enough to keep their customers happy and continue to grow revenue?

A Closer Look at Customer Loyalty

Could putting a price on customer loyalty be the answer? According to Marco Bertini, assistant professor at London Business School, it can be a distinct advantage. The following are highlights of five principles that Mr. Bertini recently shared with Harvard Business Review (HBR) on how to price goods so customers will buy them—and stay an advocate for your brand:

1. **Focus on relationships.** See your customers as people not wallets. Make sure your pricing is not merely transactional or customers are more likely to notice and respond accordingly by taking their business elsewhere. Positive approach: your company may consider bundling options versus charging for individual pieces.
2. **Be proactive.** Get to know your customers, to know what they want, and the behavior you want them to engage in. Next, set prices that will benefit both your customers and your company.

Positive approaches: Understand if your customers react more positively to a small recurring fee or to a larger one-time fee. Continue to be responsive to their customer service concerns and requests.

3. **Be flexible.** Why? Rigid pricing does not work. Since people value products differently, perfect pricing can be a moving target. The positive approach: Embrace flexible pricing, as it will help your company meet changing customer needs.
4. **Be transparent.** You will build trust and goodwill if your customers understand your pricing. Positive results: The customers you gain through transparency cost less to retain, often buy more expensive products, and are more forgiving regarding mistakes.
5. **Understand market standards.** Clarify customer perceptions of what is and what is not fair regarding pricing within your industry. Positive results: When customers believe they are paying a fair price, they are likely to buy more and pay premiums.

In Mr. Bertini's words, "Pricing is a tool that speaks loudly to customers." One parting question: What does your pricing say about your company?

OPPORTUNITY

Identify your best- and worst-selling product and/or service within the next 10 days. Now, have a small group of your best and brightest assigned to identify what the gaps are and how the gaps can be closed within the next 30 days.

IMPLEMENT

IMPACT

CHAPTER NINETEEN

Content, Clouds, and Collaboration

Have you ever wondered how safe cloud computing is and if your sensitive business content should be residing on a cloud? Or if cloud and collaborative software is a wise, long-term investment for businesses focused on growth? To find out the answers, I sat down with one of my favorite technology leaders, Paul Benjes, who is the vice president of operations at the award-winning Limelight Networks. Excerpts and valuable insight from our interview follow:

Q · Let's start from the top: Do you think the cloud and content are worth investing in?

Mr. Benjes · *Cloud and content are here to stay. It's imperative that internet communications adapt to the mobile world, which is why UC (Unified Communications) has been widely adopted among the Fortune 500 and beyond. UC Strategies encompass the next level of modality when it comes to electronic interaction; examples of this can be found with Microsoft Lync, Communicator, Salesforce.com, Chatter, Polycom's PVX software, etc.*

Q · Is no-cost content becoming a thing of the past?

Mr. Benjes · *Content has always had a fee, however, the public content such as YouTube, blip.tv, Vimeo, Hulu, and Vidler show you "user" content as free, and then hit you with advertisements and mouse-over click-throughs to entice you to go to the sponsor of that content. This also pays the* *content company whenever this video is played. The way of premium content will become more restricted and will be coupled with advertisements that are more user focused. For example, when you watch a video from "The Simpsons" on YouTube, you may have a 30-second advertisement about a video game. How did that happen? How did they know you were into video games? Cookies within your browser enable the content companies to gear ads that are most appealing to you. We will see more aggressive subscription-based pricing surrounding IP-based content as more and more content becomes digitized. The way of Cable TV and Broadcast will become a thing of the past over the next 10 years.*

Q • Will online quality content migrate behind firewalls to encourage subscription fees?

Mr. Benjes • *I struggle with this answer because online content is so readily available today through multiple media sources. In recent months we have seen a new strategy with NYT and WSJ's "teaser" content being published on Google, Bing, and Yahoo's search engines that bring you to their content, and convince you that a subscription is the best way to go. It's too early to tell for this type of content, but it is safe to say that many more companies that rely holistically on subscription services will be heading this direction. Adoption will be the biggest hurdle to overcome.*

Q • What are the advantages of clouds for businesses today? Are they economical and safe?

Mr. Benjes • *Diversity, resiliency, direct content distribution, and speed. The economics of hosting your own content and then distributing it to all of your subscribers becomes an expensive proposition. The economics of server distribution to all major ISPs is too costly to be done in today's environment and customers with large file and image requirements absolutely need to have this content sitting as close to the consumer as possible, or risk losing that customer* *to content that is more readily available. There is always a risk of safety when working in a cloud environment, so it is very important for companies in need of content distribution to work with the leaders in the Industry, the L's, the A's, and the H's of the CDN world. *Limelight, Level3, Akamai, and Highwinds are the top four CDN providers on the planet.*

Q • As far as collaboration platforms (or software), what are good examples that will stand the test of time?

Mr. Benjes • *Great examples include "Gotomeeting.com" and "Webex"; both are companies that have stood the test of time while continually improving on their technology, name brand, and services offered in the online experience. Note that they are fully adopting the UC strategies within their core business applications: Video, Audio, Web with Recording capabilities that allow for content re-distribution after an initial meeting takes place (excellent for training purposes!). There are many more platforms out there and nearly all the collaboration initiatives are attempting to use all modalities to enhance the user experience and keep the revenue "sticky." Once your product becomes commoditized, it becomes increasingly difficult to maintain market share without eroding your price. The take away: innovation must continue to consistently drive consumer interest to your business or organization.*

Q • What do you see in the future or what are you using that is working now?

Mr. Benjes • *Inexpensive and innovative things such as "Google Docs," which allow you to share the right things with the right people. This is also a direction that will set your company up for innovation in the future that goes beyond the screen with visible and audio interaction. At the time of this writing, this includes forward-thinking projects like Google Glass. The same project that arms "Google Glass Explorers" with a sophisticated pair of glasses which includes voice* *commands, basic web browsing, plus photography along with videography activated by movement.*

OPPORTUNITY

How can you encourage innovation within your company? Start by evaluating or reevaluating Goggle apps such as: Google Docs/Drive, Google Calendar, Google Chat, et al. Next, identify one collaborative platform that your company can adapt within the next 21 days to improve productivity.

IMPLEMENT

IMPACT

CHAPTER TWENTY

Ask the Expert

Is your organization looking for a way to build credibility and good will within your industry? Would it also help if this action improved search engine optimization (SEO) to your website and boosted the morale of your own talented team? If so, consider using video to showcase your organizations' experts on your home page or another primary page of your website.

Who is watching?

Three additional reasons to invest in video for the future: videos generally rank better than your organization's website; videos encourage people to stay on your website longer; and, according to comScore, 182.5 million U.S. Internet users watched 39.3 billion online content videos in March 2013.

What is industry doing?

To see examples, look no further than the high-growth industry of health care. Two worth reviewing include: Mayo Clinic's health tip library and Banner Health's expert series. First, Mayo Clinic has a dedicated section under multimedia that leads visitors through helpful stretches for the workplace with Mayo staff and patients illustrating movement. Next, Banner Health has an extensive health library featuring staff experts that discuss over 20 topics that touch our active lives. Best practice: both organizations have experts addressing frequently asked questions (FAQs) in concise videos that positively impact revenue and improve credibility while boosting their website's position.

From an investment standpoint, recent studies from comScore and others indicate that using professionally produced content with user-generated videos delivers a strong synergy in driving sales effectiveness, which is stronger than when they are used separately. This is positive news for those working with different size budgets throughout the year.

OPPORTUNITY

Which expert or product will your business highlight on video within the next two months?

IMPLEMENT

____

____

____

____

____

____

____

____

IMPACT

UNITED STATES
OF AMERICA
FEDERAL RESERVE NOTE
AB 63091815 W
B2
THIS NOTE IS LEGAL TENDER
FOR ALL DEBTS, PUBLIC AND PRIVATE
SERIES
1996
FRANKLIN
AB 63091815 W
Secretary of the Treasury
DB 86054019 A
Treasurer of the United States

CHAPTER TWENTY-ONE

Marketing Rebound: 108 Verbs That Continue to Persuade Across Platforms

According to Vizu, a Nielsen company, and the CMO Council, 2013 marks a shift in online advertising for marketers—to bigger budgets, sounder metrics, and a continuing focus on brand advertising that we identified last year.

The Numbers

In 2013, advertisers project brand ad spending to grow more quickly than direct response. Sixty-three percent of marketers project that the dollars allocated to online brand advertising will grow in 2013, and 1 in 5 believes the increase will exceed 20%.

The Right Words

Leo Burnet, legendary advertising executive, has been quoted as saying, "Dull and exaggerated ad copy is due to excess use of adjectives." To prove it, he asked his staff to compare the number of adjectives in 62 ads that failed, to the number of adjectives in Lincoln's Gettysburg Address, and other age-old classics.

The results: Of the 12,758 words in the 62 failed ads, 24.1% were adjectives. By direct comparison, Lincoln's Gettysburg Address contains only 35 adjectives out of 268 immortal words—an only 13.1% adjective-to-total-word ratio. Winston Churchill's famous Blood, Sweat and Tears speech rates even lower and has a 12.1% adjective ratio (81 adjectives from 667 words).

Mr. Burnett found that similar ratios applied to the great works such as

The Lord's Prayer, the Ten Commandments, and the Preamble to the U.S. Constitution. Conclusion: Use more verbs, not adjectives. Why? Verbs increase the pulling-power and believability of ad copy.

All good reasons to keep the 108 persuasive check sheet close at hand whenever you begin to draft the next advertisement, sales letter, website, or marketing campaign for your business.

Abolish	Defuse	Increase	Respond
Accelerate	Deliver	Innovate	Retain
Achieve	Deploy	Inspire	Save
Act	Design	Intensify	Scan
Adopt	Develop	Lead	Segment
Align	Diagnose	Learn	Shatter
Anticipate	Discover	Leverage	Shave-off
Apply	Drive	Manage	Sidestep
Assess	Eliminate	Master	Simplify
Avoid	Ensure	Maximize	Solve
Boost	Establish	Measure	Stimulate
Break	Evaluate	Mobilize	Stop
Bridge	Exploit	Motivate	Stretch
Build	Explore	Overcome	Succeed
Burn	Filter	Penetrate	Supplement
Capture	Finalize	Persuade	Take
Change	Find	Plan	Train
Choose	Focus	Position	Transfer
Clarify	Foresee	Prepare	Transform
Comprehend	Gain	Prevent	Understand
Confront	Gather	Profit	Unleash
Connect	Generate	Raise	Use
Conquer	Grasp	Realize	Whittle-down
Convert	Identify	Reconsider	Win
Create	Ignite	Reduce	
Cross	Illuminate	Refresh	
Decide	Implement	Replace	
Define	Improve	Resist	

OPPORTUNITY

Which of the 108 persuasive words can improve your next advertisement, sales letter, website, or marketing campaign?

IMPLEMENT

IMPACT

CHAPTER TWENTY-TWO

Connecting in a Virtual World

Many of us are living in the always-on age. At times, we may even text while we walk. So, what has this meant for our careers and businesses? Growth and flexibility for those who have embraced certain technology? Definitely. Specifically, it is clear that meeting clients, colleagues, and partners has taken on a new dimension, now that Skype, FaceTime, and webinars are becoming popular tools for collaboration. To uncover what is working well inside the beloved pet industry, which enjoys consistent year-over-year growth, I had the pleasure of interviewing Paula Mosteller, to learn what is behind their company's expansion. Ms. Mosteller, co-founder of PetExec, a global company that offers web-based solutions for pet daycares, shares the following insights.

Q · Is connecting with business clients in a virtual world more commonplace?

Ms. Mosteller · *Yes. For our business, connecting to clients virtually is critical. Since our product is web-*

based, we have the opportunity to share our product with potential or current clients via our browser on an international scale. Here's a recent example: on Friday in the U.S.A.—Saturday on the client's day—we present to groups in Australia who are calling in from different locations.

The news gets better: web meetings have become so advanced that even with the distance between countries, there is no noticeable communication or browser delay. To optimize our virtual connections, we prefer using a landline and a web-based product such as Fuze Meeting by FuzeBox®.

Q • What are the advantages of connecting virtually (web/video conf) in businesses today? Are they economical and safe for businesses of all sizes?

Ms. Mosteller • *Tremendous advantages for any kind of business where you can present your product or service over the web. We can connect virtually with a client in just a few seconds or plan the meeting in advance. It as if they were sitting at a computer right next to us as we point out features and benefits. The economic advantages are extreme since we can present to a potential client in Canada for an hour and a few minutes later connect to a new potential client in Texas. The ability to present in this way is absolutely critical to our growing business. Another example of savings includes streamlining new business opportunities. For instance, during a web meeting, our client and our company can both draw conclusions on whether the product and the client's business goals are a good match. Best case, we can demonstrate, sign on, and begin implementation of a software solution in the same day for our global clients. Worst case, our clients and our company have both limited the time investment to an hour, rather than a traditional alternative, which may have included travel and associated time allocated to support various evaluation meetings.*

Q • As far as web/video conference platforms (or software), what are good examples that will stand the test of time?

Ms. Mosteller • *We currently invest in Fuze Meeting. Users can connect to a client via the web with either VOIP, Skype, or landline. We also like that it works well with Mac platforms and have apps on our iPads to enhance schedule availability.*

Q · What are three other resources that your company monitors to stay in a position of growth?

Ms. Mosteller · *In order of importance: 1. Our clients – We have learned to reach out on a regular basis and ask them for ideas. We also stay connected with clients through scheduled meetings, correspondence, and social media, which gives us great insight into their businesses across the globe. 2. Industry-specific user groups such as Yahoo Groups. 3. Our partners – which provide creative ideas and extend our knowledge base, so that we are ready for the future.*

OPPORTUNITY

Who can you virtually connect with this week to streamline a business opportunity or relationship? Identify one leader at a business or organization that your company considers a key customer and schedule a virtual meeting.

IMPLEMENT

IMPACT

Ideas

CHAPTER TWENTY-THREE

Five Ways To Build Business with Current Clients

The personal touch combined with excellent client service has built today's most successful businesses and can do the same for your company. Here are five ways to develop a lasting relationship that will add value to your business on many levels:

1. **Spread the word.** Let your clients know what you're doing for them. This can be through an e-newsletter, via select press releases, a traditional newsletter, or it could be more informal by picking up the phone and calling to touch base. Regardless of the method you use, remember to point out to clients the excellent service you are providing them.
2. **Share information.** Have you read a new book, spotted an article, or heard about an association a client might be interested in? Send them a quick note or give them a call to let them know.
3. **Recognize special occasions.** Remember to send regular client birthday cards, anniversary cards, holiday cards, et al. Thoughtful gifts can be excellent follow-up options also. It is not necessary to spend a fortune to show you care; use your creativity and if time is tight, test the waters with something as simple as an electronic greeting from Hallmark.
4. **Follow up on client service issues.** Voice mail, e-mail, and even Twitter make it easy to communicate, but the personal touch can be lost. If you're having trouble getting through to a client

who's issue requires that personal contact, leave a voice-mail message that you want to talk to the client directly or will stop by his or her office at a specific time.

5. **Reconnect with old clients.** Take out the pen and write your clients from the past a personal, handwritten note. Carve out time when you find yourself on a flight, train ride, or waiting for a business meeting to begin and spend a few minutes reaching out. Another opportunity might include running into an old client at an event. This is a chance to follow up with a simple note: "It was wonderful seeing you at the holiday party. I'll call you early in the New Year to schedule a lunch."

In the end, staying connected with your clients is one of most strategic investments of time that can be made.

OPPORTUNITY

Identify how you or your leaders will connect with the business's top five clients this week. Make sure a connection is made with each of them in the next seven days.

IMPLEMENT

____

____

____

____

____

____

____

IMPACT

AÑEJO
CRUZ®
DEL SOL
HECHO EN MEXICO
100% DE AGAVE
AÑEJO
TEQUILA
40% ALC. VOL.
CONT.NET. 750 ml

CHAPTER TWENTY-FOUR

For the Love of Tequila

What happens when an established brand joins forces with a growing spirit company that is focused on quality? They break sales records and become a beloved national brand.

Encouraged by this success story, I asked the leaders of CRUZ Tequila to join a round-table discussion that gives a rare look at this award-winning business. Here is an introduction to the leadership team and what they had to say:

Mr. Pep Katcher, President

Mr. Todd Nelson, Vice President Marketing

Mr. Saulo Katcher, Vice President Operations

Mr. Todd Ellinwood, National Brand Manager

Q • **What is the history behind CRUZ Tequila?**

Mr. Todd Nelson • *My partners and I met 25 years ago when we were in college. Fast forward to 2005; while we were sharing a bottle of tequila together, my partners started exchanging stories about spending their summers in the Los Altos region of Jalisco, Mexico—which is the epicenter for ultra-premium tequila production. The bottle we had that night turned out to be pretty terrible, and someone remarked, "I bet WE could make better tequila than this."*

Mr. Saulo Katcher • *So, I picked up the phone went inside to call our cousin Ramon and ask him what it would* *take to make our own tequila. Since Ramon works in the tequila industry, he told me that he would be happy to introduce us to distillers in the area—if we were serious. I came back outside and told the group that we had an "in" down in Mexico.*

Mr. Pep Katcher • *From that point we spent the evening trying a variety of tequilas and while we appreciated the different flavor profiles, none of the tequilas had all the elements we wanted. The turning point: by the end of the evening, we knew what that ideal tequila would be.*

Mr. Saulo Katcher • *My brother, Todd Nelson, and I kept kicking the idea around. Four weeks later we decided to take Ramon up on his offer and made the journey to Mexico. As we were talking with distillers down there, all of them had product to sell us, but we needed to find a distiller who could translate our vision into a real product, rather than simply providing us with a commodity which they mass produced.*

Mr. Todd Nelson • *From the first trip, we knew we could make our own tequila and we estimated it would take us one year. However, it ended up taking us three years to develop the unique flavor profile for CRUZ Tequila. After eight years and dozens of international awards, we think it was worth it.*

Mr. Pep Katcher • *As crazy as the story may seem, it is really part of Saulo's and my childhood. Having been born in Guadalajara and then growing up in North Dakota, we still spent our summers down in Mexico. Although the summers were too short, we created memories which will last a lifetime.*

Q • **What have you done and/or do to produce the best tequila to import?**

Mr. Saulo Katcher • *Rather than importing someone else's tequila, we decided to make our own, as we wanted to make CRUZ, an exceptionally, smooth tequila, with a unique,* *softer flavor profile, which is very different from most tequilas on the market.*

Q • Where do you produce your tequila?

Mr. Pep Katcher • *Our distillery is in the highlands, near the town of Arrandas, Jalisco, Mexico. All tequila is made in Mexico, under the authority of the CRT (Consejo Regulador del Tequila), which licenses production of all tequila.*

Q • What makes a place ideal to obtain tequila?

Mr. Saulo Katcher • *Most of the premium tequilas are made in the highlands (Los Altos) of Jalisco, because of the better climate and soil conditions, which translates into better agave. There are also more craft distillers who take great pride in producing a high-quality product.*

Q • What characteristics make up good tequila?

Mr. Todd Nelson • *For CRUZ Tequila, it has always been about focusing on quality control in every aspect of production. From better agave, time-intensive slow cooking the agave, natural fermentation, and distillation.*

Q • What are the challenges of creating new ways to find/manufacture tequila?

Mr. Pep Katcher • *Tequila can only be made from the Weber Blue Agave plant, under the authority of the CRT, and only in specific parts of Mexico. It is similar to making champagne, in that you can only call it champagne if it is made in that part of France.*

Q • What areas of Arizona do you serve?

Mr. Todd Ellinwood • *CRUZ Tequila is served in over 1,100 establishments across the state of Arizona. You can find CRUZ in many of the finer dining establishments, resorts, several of the grocery stores, liquor store chains, as well as convenience and independent stores.*

Q • Is your tequila specific to Arizona?

Mr. Todd Ellinwood • *Arizona was our first state. Following our partnership with Trinchero Family Estates, our folio of spirits will be available in each of the 50 states before July 24, 2013, which is National Tequila Day in the U.S. For our fans (a.k.a., CRUZaders) outside of North America, CRUZ Tequila can be purchased online and shipped to their homes.*

Q • What are the techniques you use to specially market your tequila brand?

Mr. Todd Ellinwood • *We do a little bit of everything, from traditional mass media to event marketing to social media. CRUZ has thousands of fans and followers on Facebook and Twitter.*

Q • What makes your tequila different from the rest?

Mr. Saulo Katcher • *Besides being an Arizona company, CRUZ has a very light, soft taste. You can sip it straight and it is amazing in a margarita. Our site, CRUZTequila.com, has several interesting recipes, including the award-winning Cucumber Margarita and a delicious Watermelon Margarita.*

Q • What types of tequila do you sell?

Mr. Pep Katcher • *We currently offer three in our family of spirits, which include: CRUZ Silver, a 100% blue agave blanco tequila; CRUZ Reposado, a 100% blue agave, which is aged six months in American oak whiskey barrels; together with our much anticipated, CRUZ Anejo tequila, which recently entered the market and it is aged for over a year.*

Q • What are you plans for the summer/fall seasons? Festivals? Tequila competitions, et al.?

Mr. Todd Ellinwood • *Throughout the year, CRUZ Tequila will participate in thousands of events across North*

America. Looking at the Arizona schedule, we covered 250 tasting events during the last year, many of which are affiliated with local, worthy charities. As Cinco de Mayo nears and National Tequila Day gets closer, CRUZ Tequila has previously sponsored worthy events, including: Arizona Bike Week, CRUZCruise, Agave on the Rocks, Tequilazona, Mcdowell Mountain Music Festival, Yelp events, Splash Bash, Viva Las Vegas, and many more Tequila tasting events.

Q • What has been one of the smartest investments that CRUZ Tequila has made?

Mr. Todd Nelson • *Bringing in outside experts, investors, and advisors periodically. Why? When we have our heads down focused on the daily needs of running the business, it is difficult to pull back and look at those turning-point moments to keep leaping forward. For our leadership team, bringing in outside experts has allowed us to tell our story and discuss where we want to go. We do this with a group of trusted advisors that can bring a fresh set of eyes and make suggestions that you might not get on your own.*

OPPORTUNITY

How can you change the game, while you are playing it?

IMPLEMENT

____

____

____

____

IMPACT

Ideas

CHAPTER TWENTY-FIVE

Global Etiquette: Seven Rules That Build Business Outside of North America

Strategy and expansion are terms of endearment in business, once again. This is a positive shift, which has business leaders evaluating Mexico. Today's Mexico: a growing country the World Bank is ranking thirteenth among largest economies in nominal terms and eleventh in purchasing power. Intrigued by these statistics? If your organization is looking beyond the border for expansion opportunities, join me as I interview Melissa Lamson, a global insider you need to know. Her credentials, which include recognized author, international speaker; and award-winning business executive, have sent her on assignment across 40 countries in addition to Mexico.

Q · Ms. Lamson, to orient the audience on your industry reach, can you give us insight into which global organizations you have been working with?

Ms. Lamson · *Definitely, I have had the pleasure of working with leaders at Cisco, LinkedIn, Lufthansa, MTV, Porsche, and several other organizations, to develop global mindsets—while bridging communication across cultures. In between traveling to the next destination, I have authored three books: 7 Keys to Understanding German Business Culture, #Cultural Transformation Tweet with Advice from Silicon Valley Business Leaders, and my next book that comes out in September of this year, Why European Companies Fail in the US Market and How Yours Can Succeed.*

Q • **How important is business etiquette today? Can you give us an example or two, of when it improved the bottom line for your clients?**

Ms. Lamson • *Good business etiquette is critical. Here are two examples: first, a large Information Technology (IT) firm, based in Europe, was having retention problems in their Indian subsidiary, when they realized that the expectation was that celebrating successes was quite normal in India in business; even extended families were invited to the firm to socialize and celebrate with the employees. Retention has significantly increased and the firm is able to recruit more successfully as the subsidiary grows. Next, in the Middle East, it's critical to drink tea when offered; it's a sign of respect and trust-building, and shows your willingness to build a relationship before getting down to business. An oil company in the US called their joint venture success, "The tea party," when they signed a deal for over $250 million.*

Q • **If you had a client expanding their business in a region such as Mexico, what are seven business etiquette rules that they could start using right away?**

Ms. Lamson •

1. *Engage a trusted, mutual person, to make introductions. This action can ease uncertainty, that could slow or end initial business discussions.*
2. *Realize that Mexicans may not make eye contact during initial meetings. Why? This is a sign of respect and should not be taken as an affront. As a reminder, standing with your hands on your hips suggests aggressiveness, and keeping your hands in your pockets is impolite.*
3. *Emphasize trust, by shaking hands while exchanging verbal promises before finalizing the details in a contract or business agreement. As a reminder, men will shake*

hands upon meeting and departure and may wait for a woman to be the first to offer her hand.

4. *Established in a business relationship? Remember to socialize, get to know the person, ask questions about where they're from, and discuss what they care about outside of work. Generally, business lunches or working breakfasts, rather than dinners are the preferred form of entertainment. They are an essential part of business, which will help build a personal relationship.*
5. *Secure an optimal time for business appointments, which is between 10:00 a.m. and 1:00 p.m. with the late afternoon as a second choice.*
6. *Understand that gift giving to business leaders is not required. Although small items with branding for an initial visit are appreciated. If flowers are appropriate, keep in mind that: yellow – represents death; red – cast spells; and white – lift spells. Avoid giving gifts made of silver, as they may be associated with trinkets sold to tourists.*
7. *Focus on positive topics of conversation (after business meetings wrap up) that include: Mexican history, art, culture and museums. Topics to avoid include: earthquakes, crime, and the Mexican-American war.*

OPPORTUNITY

Has your company expanded or considered growing outside of North America? Or does your company have a global workforce? If the answer is yes to any of these scenarios, identify three business etiquette-related opportunities for improvement and implement them within the next 30 days.

IMPLEMENT

IMPACT

Ideas

CHAPTER TWENTY-SIX

Green Business

Who are the greenest companies in America? Follow along as we take a closer look at Newsweek's fourth annual report. Approach: Review the largest 500 American companies, comparing their environmental footprint, corporate management and transparency, to find which are the most eco-friendly. To conduct the study, Newsweek partnered with two leading environmental research organizations, Trucost and Sustainalytics. In addition, the methodology was developed in consultation with an advisory panel of corporate sustainability experts.

The result: one of the most comprehensive rankings available in this area and at the time of this writing. View the spotlights of best practices that follow and can be adapted now.

No. 1 · IBM

Industry: Information Technology & Services

NEWSWEEK Green Score: 82.9

IBM's "Smarter Planet" products help clients measure and reduce their resource consumption—and save money. At its Zurich lab, water that cools a supercomputer is used to warm nearby buildings.

No. 2 · Hewlett-Packard

Industry: Technology Equipment

NEWSWEEK Green Score: 78.5

HP has lowered its emissions by more than 50% since 2005, and has pushed its suppliers to get green as well, effectively refusing to work with paper companies linked to deforestation and illegal logging.

No. 3 · Sprint Nextel

Industry: Telecommunications
NEWSWEEK Green Score: 77.5
Sprint was the first telecom to collect and reuse discarded devices, and it gives online buyers credits every time they turn in their old phones. By 2017, it hopes to recycle nine of every 10 devices it sells.

No. 4 · Dell

Industry: Technology Equipment
NEWSWEEK Green Score: 77.1
The computer maker creates almost zero waste, reusing or recycling an astounding 98% of its nonhazardous by-products. It's a leader in smarter packaging, using bamboo instead of cardboard.

No. 5 · CA Technologies

Industry: Information Technology & Services
NEWSWEEK Green Score: 77.1
The management software provider lets 30% of its employees work from home, cutting back on pollution from commuting. By 2015, it plans to buy 25% of its electricity from renewable sources.

No. 6 · NVIDIA

Industry: Technology Equipment
NEWSWEEK Green Score: 76.3
It invented GPUs, the most energy-efficient computer processors on the market. And since 2007, it has diverted 85% of its waste from landfills to compost and recycling facilities.

No. 7 · Intel

Industry: Technology Equipment
NEWSWEEK Green Score: 75.2
The chip maker buys more green power than any company in

the U.S., has reduced greenhouse gas emissions by 60% since 2007, and even partially ties employee compensation to its green performance.

No. 8 • Accenture

Industry: Information Technology & Services
NEWSWEEK Green Score: 74.7
The consulting firm encourages employees to avoid nonessential travel, holding virtual conferences when possible. By 2012, employees' carbon footprints were 30% smaller than in 2007.

No. 9 • Office Depot

Industry: Retailers
NEWSWEEK Green Score: 74.4
Its "Green Fleet" employs a line of electric vans and cargo-carrying bicycles to deliver 90% of its packages in London, reducing its carbon emissions by some 60% in that city.

No. 10 • Staples

Industry: Retailers
NEWSWEEK Green Score: 74.4
The office supply chain uses solar panels at over 30 U.S. facilities, including an array of 1,727 individual panels at its Los Angeles sports arena. In 2011, it helped customers recycle 67 million ink and toner cartridges.

No. 11 • EMC

Industry: Technology Equipment
NEWSWEEK Green Score: 73.6
EMC began a "Journey to the Cloud" in 2004, moving its IT services and infrastructure to a virtual space, and saving huge amounts of energy. The company's headquarters also include a facility that treats wastewater for reuse in cooling, sanitation and irrigation.

No. 12 • Microsoft

Industry: Information Technology & Services

NEWSWEEK Green Score: 73.5

In the spring of 2012, Microsoft announced it was taking the unusual step of charging its individual divisions a "carbon fee," making each of them responsible for tracking, minimizing, and offsetting the environmental costs associated with electrical use and air travel. As a result, in the current fiscal year, the company will be carbon-neutral for the first time ever..

No. 13 • Cognizant

Industry: Information Technology & Services

NEWSWEEK Green Score: 73.1

Cognizant's "paperless offices" program has reduced paper consumption by 60% since 2008. In that time, the technology company has reduced its per capita carbon emissions by 32%, and energy consumption by 34%. And last year, its CGSearch app, which lets users compare air quality and pollutant levels across cities, won the EPA's popular choice award

No. 14 • Hartford Financial Services Group

Industry: Financials

NEWSWEEK Green Score: 72.8

The financial services company has electric vehicle charging stations at all of its Connecticut locations, and it offers discounted insurance policies to customers with hybrid or electric cars. With more than 4,000 employees taking advantage of the flexible work program by working remotely, the environmental impact of employee commutes is lessened even more.

No. 15 • McGraw-Hill

Industry: Media & Publishing

NEWSWEEK Green Score: 72.8

In 2011, more than 95% of the publisher's paper purchases (approximately 77,703 metric tons) came through suppliers adhering to rigorous, chain-of-custody forest certification, meaning the paper was produced in the most environmentally sustainable way possible.

OPPORTUNITY

Does your company have a sustainability or eco-friendly business plan in place that could be refreshed? Is your company looking at building a plan or created processes in this area? If the answer is yes to either of these scenarios, identify three business strategies for improvement and implement them within the next 30 days.

IMPLEMENT

IMPACT

DO NOT CROSS
SCENE
CROSS

CHAPTER TWENTY-SEVEN

Deadly Consequences: Houston We Have a Problem

What if today was not just another day in the office—what if an active shooter was in your building? Would you run, hide, or fight to save your life? More importantly, what should you do?

To answer these questions, the city of Houston has released a video entitled "Run. Hide. Fight. Surviving an Active Shooter Event" that provides advice. At the time of this writing, the six-minute reel has captured over one million views on YouTube.com, has been created with a U.S. Homeland Security grant, and suggests actions to take if you are confronted by a shooter. To be clear, the video depicts violence and it may be unsettling to some people. However, the reality of a sudden, violent incident is not pleasant.

In addition to the "Run. Hide. Fight." video, the city of Houston used the grant for research. They also ran an exercise involving local first responders, state and federal authorities, together with companies, stated Jessica Michan, a spokesperson for the Mayor's office, whom a Bloomberg journalist interviewed recently. During this active-shooter planning, the city decided to produce the video and other written material to educate citizens on tips to protect themselves during such an event.

Hesitation Can Be Deadly

According to corporate security experts in Arizona, the one thing that anyone can do to help ensure his or her safety is to be mentally prepared to respond in the unlikely event of an attack. Why? Because the single, most common reaction to an active-shooter is: disbelief. The same disbelief that can produce a delay in responding as the brain attempts to process the situation. A delay—that could lead to tragedy.

Awareness and Prevention

It is clear from recent headlines that the fast-paced world we live in does occasionally feel more like an action movie than reality. Also stress, angry people, and team conflict can cause risk to organizations. So what can you do today, to work toward a safer workplace for tomorrow?

For guidance, I spoke with Ms. Fredrickson, a law enforcement veteran, specializing in emergency services and disaster preparedness. "The best way to reduce workplace violence is to educate employees to recognize and report warning signs and red flags of workplace violence," adds Carol Fredrickson, co-founder of Violence Free, a firm with headquarters in Arizona. "Today the investments that our North American and Canadian clients make in their organizations, are focused on preventing 6–7 figure lawsuits and more importantly, averting violent workplace disasters."

OPPORTUNITY

What steps will your organization take to heighten awareness and prevent a sudden, violent incident from erupting?

IMPLEMENT

____

____

____

____

IMPACT

Rolls Out

CHAPTER TWENTY-EIGHT

Risky Business

In business, bumps in the road can occur and smart companies plan for this. Two successful strategies that will stand the test of time: assemble a pre-determined team of experts that your company would need if a worst-case scenario presented itself and next, build key messages that address the situation in a concise, appropriate manner.

Further, your experts may include but not be limited to: lawyer(s), secondary supplier(s), emergency IT focal point(s), web services, medical/psychological organizations or media relation experts, depending on which industry or field your company is in.

If your company is looking for qualified experts in any of the fields listed above, here are four resources worth a review: 1) The Better Business Bureau, 2) Business Journal Book of List (in 60 US markets), 3) U.S. Chamber of Commerce, and for those companies who actively support the critical small business sector, 4) The Small Business Administration has good resources.

OPPORTUNITY

Build your risk management team of experts. Do you already have one in place? Set aside time to evaluate the team members and key messages, to make sure they complement the current business objectives.

IMPLEMENT

IMPACT

Ideas

CHAPTER TWENTY-NINE

Can We Avoid Office Politics?

Seasoned leaders have survived their fair share of political drama. The reality: politics can be a killer of productivity and even careers, in the most extreme cases. So how can leaders of all ages avoid them?

For answers, let's take a look at Karen Dillon's guide for Harvard Business Review titled "Office Politics," which can keep us from crossing over to the dark side.

> **Scenario One · It Looks Like A Clique – How can you gain influence when the cool leaders band together?**
>
> **Background:** Office cliques form—and thrive—for lots of reasons. Sometimes, for instance, you'll find bands of colleagues who have moved together from other companies or organizations, particularly in industries that are worlds unto themselves, such as media and technology. (And it makes sense: As leadership expert Herminia Ibarra points out, research consistently shows that the key to getting a new job is networking.) When people know one another socially or from past jobs, they naturally have stronger, deeper ties.
>
> **How to adapt:** A – Work with the existing clique. Don't let the golden children get all the heat and light.
>
> Even if you're not invited to contribute to their big projects, express interest in them. Leadership consultant Ron Ashkenas advises, "You can say to your boss or colleagues, 'I know I'm not on that assignment, but could I sit in on a status meeting

to learn more about it?'" And once you're in the room, offer to pitch in. B – Form your own alliances or coalitions. Maybe chumminess at the office feels artificial to you or seems like a waste of time. You may be thinking, Why put aside my "real" work just to make friends? But the reality is, it'll help you do your work more effectively. First, you'll gain support for your ideas. No matter how respected you might be individually, you'll always bolster your case by lining up allies.

Scenario Two • Big Bad Bully – Can you change the dynamic?

Background: Bullies are more prevalent then we once thought, according to a study by Christine Pearson at the Thunderbird School of Global Management in Arizona and Christine Porath at Georgetown University's McDonough School of Business: 78% of participants who believed they'd been treated rudely by colleagues said they felt a decreased commitment to their work, with a direct negative effect on their performance. You—and your work—don't have to suffer.

How to adapt: A – Consider the bullies' intentions. Some bullies don't mean to be bullies. So make sure you aren't projecting a motive that isn't there. B – Offer an olive branch. Disarm your bully by expressing your desire to have a good relationship with them. C – Find safety in numbers. Although you don't want to create a rival gang to counter the office bully, there is power in people banding together to support one another publicly. D – Break the pattern. How do you put an end to this destructive dance? The easiest thing to change is your own behavior.

Scenario Three • Time For The Office Outing – Forcing the fun factor or looking through a networking lens?

Background: Your company has a couple of splashy employee events each year—and that kind of "forced fun" is not your cup of tea. You like most of your colleagues, but you dread the thought of trust falls, or pelting one another with paint balls, or laughing politely at your colleague's colorful jokes over charred burgers and potato salad. You'd rather skip it, but everyone is expected to attend, so your absence would be duly noted.

How to adapt: A – Find a comfortable way to participate. If you're fortunate, you welcome the opportunity to hang out with your coworkers because you're fond of them. However, even if that's not the case, says leadership coach Susan Alvey, a principal at Pemberton Coaching, assume the most positive perspective you can. "Instead of looking for the first moment to escape, think about how you can have a good time." B – Focus on connecting. View the outing as a personal-growth exercise, Clark advises: "Use it to hone one of the most talked about, but least practiced, skills in corporate life: asking questions that draw people out and then really listening to their answers." C – Don't check your inhibitions at the door. Of course, as you're trying to relax and be yourself, you'll want to maintain some sense of decorum. We're all adults—and most of us know our limits—yet we've all seen people have too many drinks at office events. D – If you mess up, take responsibility for your actions. So what if you wake up the following morning and realize that you may have crossed the line at the office party? "If you do something embarrassing, own up to it," Alvey says. You don't need to send out a mass e-mail to everyone in the company. But have the courage to apologize to anyone who witnessed your behavior.

OPPORTUNITY

What political issue can you tackle in the next 10 days? Identify and address one issue. Follow this action with a quick evaluation on how the solution positively impacted your interactions with fellow leaders or business colleagues.

IMPLEMENT

IMPACT

Ideas

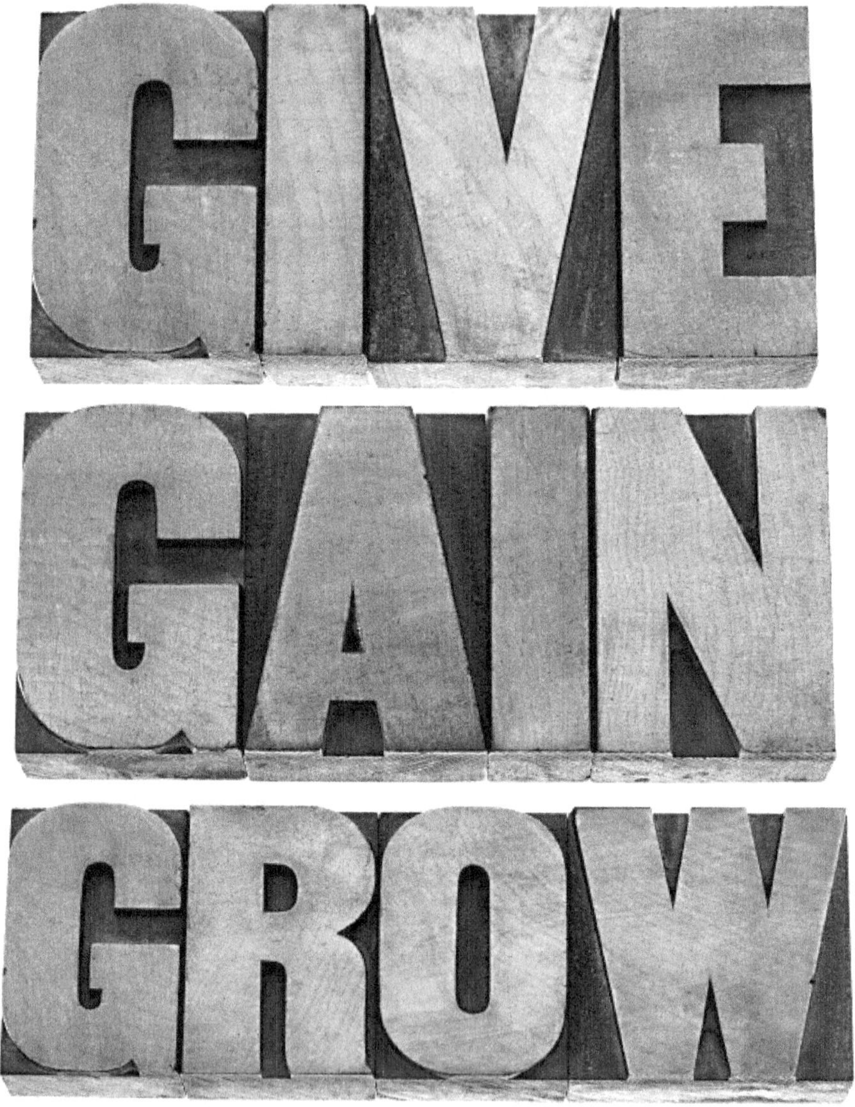

GIVE

GAIN

GROW

CHAPTER THIRTY

Paying It Forward and Adapt Now

On a personal note, giving back and paying it forward have been important actions that this leader has taken throughout my career. In both good and challenging economies, it has been important to me and will continue. To that end, a portion of *Adapt Now* book proceeds will be donated to FEED USA through 2015.

It is also an honor to tell you that each of the leaders interviewed for *Adapt Now* gives back in many different ways and across a number of charities that are making a difference in the world we live in.

Join us.

Packing Tips for Busy Leaders

It is true, we all know savvy globetrotters who instinctively travel with less and for many years this leader did not fall into that category. However, I have learned over time, the value of traveling with a carryon roller board and the flexibility it affords when connecting in the world largest airports. To that end, here are nine packing strategies that work:

1. **Look ahead**
   Is this a business trip that dictates you will dress to impress? Or will you be visiting operational sites where business casual clothing is the order of the day? As your itinerary comes together, make a schedule of your days and evenings, and next to each activity note potential outfits, including shoes and accessories. This will help you determine your clothing needs for the trip.
2. **The list**
   In a Fodor's survey, 29% of respondents said they make lists at least one week before a trip. Looking for a standard list? Check out Knock Knock's clever 'Pack This!' note pads (on-line and at Amazon) that this leader uses for each trip. Remember, lists can be used at least twice - once to pack and once to repack at the end of your trip. This way you'll be sure to take everything you've brought with you.
3. **From point a to point b**
   Remember, you have to get there from here. A powerful reminder - for anyone who loves fashion and large suite cases.

Further, if there's one thing that can turn a pack rat into a minimalist, it's a business trip spent lugging everything you've packed over long distances. Consider how you're getting to your ONEdestination and how you'll be getting around once you arrive. Packing light is less critical on trips when you're driving with your colleagues and staying in one place than when you're flying on an airplane and moving around once you land.

4. **Looking good**

   It goes without saying that you should never leave on a trip without broken-in (polished) shoes. Similarly, don't run out and buy a new wardrobe. You will probably want to wear each item you bring several times during your trip, so you're better off with clothing you know and love - clothes that are comfortable and make you feel good.

5. **It is a custom**

   Local dress codes should be factored into your wardrobe. In some resort areas, an anything-goes attitude applies, whereas in others many restaurants frown on diners with flip flops or those wearing shorts, bathing suits, or even T-shirts. Going abroad? In many places, traditions of dress differ from North America; check with your destination's concierge or consult a good guidebook. A dignified look goes a long way: think skirts below the knee or trousers, and shirts that cover shoulders and elbows.

6. **Do the math**

   You can pack fewer items if you will be staying in one place long enough to have laundry and dry cleaning done during your trip. You'll have to pack more if you'll be moving at a dead run for most of your journey, changing hotels every day, or if you don't trust the quality of the local laundries and dry cleaners to handle the clothes you want to take.

7. **One look**

   Stick to one basic wardrobe look – a favorite is urban chic. Also sporty casual – if a visit to an operations site is on the agenda.

In either case, choose clothes that you can wear at least twice in a week. When all your tops go with all your bottoms and all your bottoms work with all your shoes, mixing and matching can yield plenty of fresh looks; just add scarves and jewelry for women and additional ties along with a light weight sweater or blazer for men (e.g., for a week's trip, you should look smashing with three bottoms, four or five tops, a sweater, and a jacket that can be worn alone or over the sweater.)

8. **Colors and practicality are key**

Similarly, try to build your wardrobe around just two or three complementary colors, preferably two neutrals and one accent, such as black, white, and light brown. If everything goes together, you'll get more mileage out of fewer pieces. And remember that prints and dark colors do not show spots and soil as quickly. Think black T-shirts rather than white ones and apply this to pants as well.

As much as is possible, pack items that are lightweight, wrinkle resistant, worth repeating – wrinkle resistant, compact, and washable. Slimmer silhouettes, for instance, will generally pack tighter than flared or ruffled looks. Clothes made of fabric with built-in wrinkles tend to travel beautifully, while lightweight linen creases to the point you will not want to wear it. Try this simple wrinkling test: Intentionally fold a piece of fabric between your fingers for a couple of minutes. If it refuses to crease, it will probably come out of your suitcase looking fresh. Another important tip: use tissue paper and dry cleaning bags when packing your most important outfits.

9. **Sunny and 70 degrees**

Start checking the temperatures for your destination a week before your trip. Having current weather information allows you to revise your packing list appropriately and to consider buying sunscreen, insect repellent, pack layers (a favorite tip of mine), or whatever else you may need for the weather. If rain is in the forecast, avoid suede finishes and opt for easy to clean boots, heels, or loafers. And be sure to consider the humidity level which could translate into packing hair clips or hats.

OPPORTUNITY

Before your next business trip: start a list 7 days in advance, check the weather of the destination, and leave for the trip with less wardrobe headaches. Already a good packer? Share your number one tip with a newer colleague or family member - before they take off on their next trip.

IMPLEMENT

IMPACT

APPENDIX TWO

On The Move

Looking for a resource designed with movers and shakers in mind? Start with the Business Journal's automated 'People On the Move' system. Whether it is for you or those on your team, It remains complimentary plus it allows for these announcements: new employees, promotions, recognition, and Board of Directors.

Additional benefits: this family of publications reach 41 different markets across the U.S.; when you share the good news on-line, remember it could be added to print versions of the Business Journal's; and there is the potential to improve search engine optimization if you reference website(s) in the announcement.

Living near New York or Chicago? Look into Crain's Business on-line publication. They also offer 'On the Move' sections that you or your team can use to acknowledge: new employees, promotions, recognition, and changes to Board members.

OPPORTUNITY

Each month schedule a meeting with the leadership team to identify what announcements surrounding: new employees, promotions, recognition, along with changes to Board members should be released (internally/externally) and issue the news.

IMPLEMENT

IMPACT

Ideas

APPENDIX THREE

What To Include In Today's Press Kit

What are the key elements of a press kit that Producers will hang on to?

A Look Inside

1. Introduction using a concise summary in an Associate Press 'about' statement format
2. Press releases that include current and past news. Positive reprints are also great additions
3. Images and logos are important. If you have hard and electronic press kits make sure your team has high resolution digital images and logos that can be sent out easily to the media
4. Endorsements and quotes from leadership, along with any third parties (e.g., outlining benefits & value)
5. Bios of leadership and/or an organizational summary that is cleared for external audiences. Professional headshots (high resolution, digital format) of the leadership team should also be available.

The When And The Who

- Building on strategic partnerships
- Growing membership and enhancing sponsorship discussions
- Participating in conferences together with industry and community events

- Responding to media inquiries and interview opportunities
- Evaluating/interviewing new potential leaders and management candidates
- Supporting media outreach efforts to new editors or journalist

OPPORTUNITY

Within the next two weeks set up a meeting with your marketing or PR team to take a close look at the businesses press kits. If your business does not have a press kit, set a timeline to get one built and put a plan in place to make sure that annual updates will be made.

IMPLEMENT

____

____

____

____

____

____

____

____

IMPACT

APPENDIX FOUR

30 Reasons To Embrace Media Outreach

Milestones, events, and news worth releasing to the wire*:

1. Starting a new business
2. Introducing a new product
3. Celebrating an anniversary
4. Announcing a restructuring of the company
5. Offering an article series for publishing
6. Opening up branch or satellite offices
7. Receiving an award
8. Receiving an appointment
9. Participating in a philanthropic event
10. Introducing a unique strategy/approach
11. Announcing a partnership
12. Changing the company or product name
13. Earning recognition of the company, product or executives by a publication
14. Announcing that you're available to speak on particular subjects of interest
15. Issuing a statement of position regarding a local, regional or national issue

16. Announcing a public appearance on television, radio or in person
17. Launching a website
18. Announcing free information available
19. Announcing that you've reached a major milestone
20. Obtaining a new, significant customer
21. Expanding or renovating the business
22. Establishing a unique vendor agreement
23. Meeting some kind of unusual challenge or rising above adversity
24. Restructuring your business or its business model
25. Setting up a customer advisory group
26. Announcing the results of research or surveys you have conducted
27. Announcing that an individual in your business has been named to serve in a leadership position in a community, professional or charitable organization
28. Sponsoring a workshop or seminar
29. Making public statements on future business trends or conditions
30. Forming a new strategic partnership or alliance

**What is a Wire? It is a company that's focuses on the direct, instantaneous delivery of your press release to an interested audience that's vast in scope, including thousands of media, bloggers and the public.*

Benefits: when you use the wire to distribute your press release, your message will be delivered to:

Media: This includes journalists and editors at newspapers, financial media, trade publications, consumer and special interest magazines, radio stations, television stations and internet news services.

Internet audiences: Targeting thousands of web sites, ranging from the internet's largest news portal to niche and local media outlets

Search engines: Another primary source of news from corporations and other organizations, wire distributor's news is incorporated into engines like Google News and Yahoo! News, and is indexed by hundreds of search engines

OPPORTUNITY

Set up time in the next 21 days to get your leadership team together, agree on the subject of a wire release and prepare to issue it early in the week to leverage visibility for your business.

IMPLEMENT

IMPACT

Ideas

APPENDIX FIVE

You've Got Email

If the average office worker spends over 26% of their workday on email, can we streamline to recover the precious commodity of time?

According to a recent McKinsey Global Institute report on "the social economy," the average knowledge worker now spends more than 26% of their work time managing email. If you work 50 hours per week, that's 14 hours stuck in the inbox. McKinsey's report suggested that workers could improve their email productivity by 25-30% through better use of social collaboration platforms, buying back 7-8.5% of their workweek. But even if your company isn't investing in such platforms, here's some low-hanging fruit for getting your head out of your inbox for a few of those 14 hours:

Automate

Embrace professional and/or branded signatures for your emails. After pointing, clicking, and the auto insert is finished – so is your sign off. This small action can save your audience significant time and effort if they need to speak with you urgently by phone as a follow up or email connections are slowing the progress toward your goal.

Take a closer look at those subscriptions

Going back to the previous analysis that included 5 million emails from Baydin, an email management service, detailing that the average email user gets 147 messages per day and deletes 71 (48%). Deletion takes an average of 3.2 seconds. Granted, that doesn't sound like much - about 4 minutes per day - but if you're deleting 350 emails per workweek, that takes around 20 minutes per week, which adds up to more than 16 hours per year.

Or look at it this way: According to the American Time Use Survey, the average married, employed father who has children under age 6 spends just 2.4 minutes per day reading to them -- which is less time than the average email user spends deleting emails. Play offense with your inbox by getting yourself off any lists you don't read, and unsubscribing to commercial messages.

Avoid using folders

One paper from Carnegie Mellon University found that over 30% of email users agree with the statement, "I file my messages into folders as soon as I have read them." Filing seems productive, but according to Alex Moore, CEO of Baydin, creating files associated with different projects or people is the least efficient way to find emails you might need again in the future - less efficient, in fact, then scrolling back through your inbox trying to remember roughly when the needed email came in. Which is exactly what this leader does 90% of the time. Solution: You can create one "archive" folder if you like to keep your inbox empty, but use the search function to find any information you need.

Check your timing

According to recent analysis, the average email user writes 40 messages a day, but there's no point writing these emails if they don't get read. A message sent at 6 a.m. is more likely to be opened than one sent later in the day, reports validate that there is also a small bump in reading after lunch. Tip: If you need to ask someone to do something, you're more likely to get what you want after their blood sugar is up

Follow these simple strategies and chances are, you'll get a lot more done.

OPPORTUNITY

In the next 7 days, identify what strategies your team will adopt in order for the company to drive change that will allow office worker to spend less than 26% of their workday on email. Bottom line: how can the company streamline the process to recover the precious commodity of time?

IMPLEMENT

IMPACT

About the Author

Kelly Isley Is a *Fortune 100* top performer who is a strategist, business leader and author with more than 20 years of experience in the aerospace, aviation, engineering, healthcare, and advertising industries. Collectively, she has helped her clients raise more than $725 million in capital, complete $550+ million in acquisitions, secure high-profile partnerships and capture 7-figure incentive programs.

During her career she has managed asset risk for program development, created reseller/manufacturing partnerships, executed award-winning communications programs, built profitable strategic plans, and managed operations teams for *Fortune 500* companies. Her demonstrated turnaround capabilities for critical programs have focused on customers throughout Europe, North America, and South America. Ms. Isley, has also co-created a corporate case study published by Thunderbird University, The American Graduate School of International Business. She is a member of the Society of Professional Journalists, International Association of Business Communicators, a recognized journalist, and licensed pilot.

CPSIA information can be obtained at www.ICGtesting.com
Printed in the USA
BVOW08*1031180614

356262BV00002B/4/P

9 780988 751804